The LONG GOODNIGHT KISS

A BBC RADIO PLAY
BY
DAVID KAYE

In Memory of

Gloria Maddox

My Original Theatrical Muse

©Copyright 1987/2013 by David Kaye
All Rights Reserved

INTRODUCTION

Writing a play for BBC Radio was not something I would have thought of by myself. When I lived in my native USA, radio drama was pretty much considered a thing of the past, something that had flourished way back in the 1930s and 1940s before it was abruptly killed off by television. But in the UK, it was still alive and well thanks primarily to the BBC and to good old British tradition. It was also easier to do radio drama on a national scale because Britain was a much smaller country. So it was the place where generations of aspiring playwrights got their first break.

Shortly after I moved to London, I got involved with a playwrights' workshop that was run by Donna Franceschild, an American writer who had lived in the UK for a number of years. At the time, she was associated with the Donmar Warehouse theatre which was a kind of London version of Off Broadway. I primarily got into the workshop because I had not written anything for several years – for a variety of reasons – and I thought that being among other writers might provide some much needed inspiration or motivation. Most of the people in the workshop had less writing experience than I had and only one had ever had a play produced, by BBC Radio. Everyone seemed to be tailoring their writing towards radio and I was intrigued by this possible new opportunity. My plays had always been more about characters and dialogue than lots of onstage action so I thought that my style might easily adapt to the medium of radio.

The workshop was an interesting experience. Each week we would do a reading from someone's work in progress then discuss it with an honesty that was not always appreciated. Other times, a member of the group would merely present a basic idea for a play and some of us would do an improvisation to explore possible ways it could develop. It all certainly got my creative juices flowing again and my writer's block soon disappeared.

My first attempt at a play written specifically for radio was the play in this book. The initial idea came from some late night banter with my new English wife and then I decided to see if I could sustain a play with just two characters for any length of time. The transition from writing a stage play to something that could only be heard took a bit of getting used to. I knew I would have to engage an audience's imagination but wanted to be careful about how information about appearances and action were presented. What I really wanted to avoid was the old "Is that a pistol in your left hand that you are pointing at me?" type of dialogue. It was a challenge but an interesting one.

Once I was satisfied with my efforts, there was only one thing to do – mail it off to the Script Department at BBC Radio. They received thousands of unsolicited scripts every year so the odds of having one accepted were low. But after waiting over six months, I got a letter from Penny Gold, a script editor who was enthusiastic about my play and was hoping to persuade a producer to take it on. Three more months passed before I was informed that my play was indeed going to be produced as part of Radio Four's *Thirty Minute Theatre* series. My play was actually a bit longer than half an hour so there was obviously going to be some cutting involved. Many more months went by before I finally got a BBC copy of the script plus all the information about the cast, director, and recording session. One change was necessary almost immediately. I had called my play *Bedtime Story* but that title was apparently already in use so I was asked to provide an alternative. Off the top of my head, I suggested *The Long Goodnight Kiss* which everyone thought was even better. (This was several years before the film *The Long Kiss Goodnight* came out.)

About eighteen months after I had first submitted my play, I arrived at Broadcasting House for the recording session. This was a huge place and, once I got past the security desk, I had no idea where to go. Luckily, the actor who was doing my play, Basil Moss, signed in at the same time and he offered to lead me down into the bowels of the building where the studios were. It was a rabbit warren of differently sized recording studios for the various BBC stations. Many had red lights outside their doors to indicate that they were either recording or broadcasting live. We eventually arrived at Studio B10 and were greeted by our director, David Johnston, and the other member of the cast, Judy Franklin. These three were obviously old friends and one of the reasons David had agreed to do the play was the chance to work with Basil and Judy again.

No sooner had we got to the studio then we all jumped into a lift to an upstairs canteen for coffee and a bit of breakfast. The others expressed their surprise that I was an American because they all felt that the play and its dialogue were very English. I admitted that this was the result of a lifetime of absorbing English books, plays, and movies, not to mention having an English wife. Judy, in particular, was full of praise for the way I had presented the female character. This view was also shared, I found out later, by our female production assistant. I was quite flattered by all this enthusiasm for my work, something I was not exactly used to.

Back in the studio, the serious work began. It was a fairly large studio with microphones set in different areas to replicate the sound of different rooms. There were various props and things like a door and a few wooden stairs that were used for sound effects. The small control booth was set above us but, to start, we all sat in a circle for a straight read through of the play with Claire, the production assistant, carefully timing it with a stopwatch. At this point, I was a mere observer but it was fascinating to hear my dialogue being acted out by these professionals. When I write a play, I usually have a different voice in my head for each character which helps me to shape the way they speak. So to hear real actors saying my words can be both a revelation and a frustration as they put their own personal spin on the characters.

Basil and Judy were both very nice but I have to admit they were not what I had in mind when I wrote the characters they were playing. I saw the couple in the play as being mid-30s, about my age at the time, but these two were easily ten to fifteen years older than that. And they both spoke with rather old-fashioned, plummy BBC accents which did not entirely match my idea of the characters. They both gave excellent performances but they were not really what I had imagined.

Once the play was read and timed, there was a discussion with David giving out various notes. As I suspected, the play ran longer than thirty minutes so some trimming would be required. David broached this subject with me as though walking on eggshells but I assured him that I could find the cuts required without upsetting the flow of the piece. I knew from my previous theatre experience that there was no such thing as a final script and that the rehearsal process was the place to edit and improve. I also knew that lines of dialogue that seemed great on paper did not always work as well when spoken aloud. So I was quite prepared to alter or tweak the script where necessary. David seemed relieved by this. He told me that the last time he had worked with a first-time radio author, he had a fifteen minute debate about changing an "and" to a "but" in the script. So he was very happy that I had a professional attitude.

David Johnston was an old pro at directing radio plays. He was a quietly flamboyant character who called me "darling" and who could not talk without moving his hands. He seemed particularly concerned about a few of the very long speeches in the play which he referred to as "arias". I told him that I was very influenced by John Osborne in my younger days and they were the result. He smiled at me like a tolerant uncle. We also discussed whether there were too many pauses in the script. "For

Gawd's sake, darling," he said, "don't go all Harold Pinter on me!" He told me that when Pinter first started as a playwright doing radio plays, he put in all those famous "Pinter pauses" to pad out the running time because he was paid by the minute.

The morning was spent rehearsing with me doing a bit of re-writing and deleting. At one point, Basil was supposed to kiss Judy but instead he kissed the back of his hand. This was an indication of how long it had been since Basil had worked in radio. The newer technology and microphones meant that he now had to kiss Judy for real, something that made him slightly embarrassed. It was also time to rehearse some of the effects. There were two kinds of sounds effect – pre-recorded ones in the booth and live ones performed by a very busy chap in the studio. He did everything from opening doors, lighting cigarettes, and rustling bedclothes. Before I knew it, it was lunchtime.

I don't know where everyone else went for lunch but I had a quick one at a nearby McDonalds then sat on the steps of All Souls Church working on a few more edits that David and I had discussed. I presented these to everyone back in the studio and David seemed very pleased. Basil, on the other hand, actually asked that a particular line from one of the "arias" be reinstated, saying "I really like that line." I took this as a great compliment and the line was put back in. Of course, I was well aware that David would have the final say when he came to edit the play into its allotted running time.

Once we had all marked the final changes in the script, David and I retreated to the control booth and the actual recording began. By this time, my work was done and I just sat and watched it all unfold in front of me. The recording was done in bits with the occasional second take when a line was flubbed or someone became tongue-tied. "I'll fix that in the editing," David kept saying to me as the engineer nodded knowingly. At one point, Judy was supposed to throw a coffee cup across the room in anger. Rather than use a sound effect, David wanted her to actually hurl a cup into a corner. Six cups were smashed to pieces before one made the sort of sound that David was looking for. After that, we took a short break because everyone was laughing so much.

Halfway through the afternoon, a BBC announcer showed up to record the opening and closing credits. He was there less than ten minutes then rushed off to perform similar tasks in other studios. Our own recording session progressed quite smoothly and the whole thing was finished slightly ahead of schedule. At the end of the play, there was supposed to be a jazz ballad. David or his assistant had found a track in the BBC library that suited the mood perfectly. I was less pleased with a single line near the end of the play which I did not recognise. Apparently, David had inserted it when the script was being prepared. It was just a short line but I felt it did not match my style and was out of character for Basil. I voiced my opinion but the line was recorded anyway. But it is not included in the script as presented here.

With the recording finished, David invited me to join him and Basil and Judy in the BBC Club for a drink. That really was a special club, busy and smoky and crowded with some recognisable faces and voices from the BBC. Judy asked me lots of questions about my writing and what I planned to write next. David sat next to me and was full of praise for my little effort. It would not hurt my future chances, I realised, to have a veteran director on my side when I submitted further scripts to Penny Gold or any of the other script editors. David was somewhat dismissive of those people. He told me that there were only two kinds of script editors at the BBC – those who had just come down from Oxford and those who had just come down from Cambridge, implying that none of them had any real life experience.

After a couple of drinks, we all went our separate ways. David and his engineer would do the final edit of the play the next day but I would have to wait until it was broadcast to hear the result. It would be two months before the play was aired and it was a bit of a thrill to see its details and synopsis listed in the *Radio Times*. The first broadcast was in the late afternoon on a weekday but it was repeated a few days later in the evening for maximum exposure. This meant that I got a 75% repeat fee for the second broadcast which gave me a tidy sum for my efforts, which paid for a lovely two week holiday in Spain the following summer.

There were no reviews or ratings for radio drama so it was difficult to know how it was received. Apparently, *Thirty Minute Theatre* had a loyal base of listeners and I was told the play was probably heard by at least a million or two. It was certainly a much larger audience than any of my stage plays ever had. I recorded the play off the radio and made copies on cassette to send to friends back in the States. Everyone said they liked it but, of course, they may have just been polite.

All in all, I was quite pleased with the final result, even with my reservations about the casting. Basil and Judy did a marvellous job and made the dialogue and characters sound real and believable. I was also amazed at how skilfully the sound effects, both live and recorded, were integrated into the play. The whole thing was a demonstration of just how good the BBC was at producing radio drama. When I decided to publish this script, I listened to the play for the first time in many years and I still felt proud of it, even though there were one or two tiny things that I wished we had done differently.

I did have a few tangible results after the broadcast. I was invited to join the Writers Guild of Great Britain which was very nice. I went to a kind of workshop there and met several well-known writers whose names I had seen on television and film credits. They were all full of encouragement and advice. Then I was asked to write some skits and song lyrics for a charity show that was staged at the Duchess Theatre in London which I could more or less regard as my West End debut. I was also approached by a German radio station who wanted to translate and broadcast *The Long Goodnight Kiss* which I somehow could not imagine being done in that language.

My relationship with BBC Radio over the next few years was a very up and down affair – nothing is ever as good as the first time. My efforts were a combination of new material and adaptations of plays I had written for the stage. It all fizzled out when the BBC decided to air a radio soap opera two or three times a week which took away some of the air time previously devoted to original plays, then they had a series of budget cuts which further reduced the number of plays being produced. My favourite script editor Penny Gold moved on to other things and David Johnston retired. With the market for plays, radio or otherwise, rapidly drying up, I decided to concentrate instead on writing books. But that is another story.

The play is presented here in its full and original version, before all the minor cuts and edits. I have incorporated the various stage directions and sound effect notes from the working script.

David Kaye
September 2013

The Long Goodnight Kiss

was first broadcast on BBC Radio Four

on September 1, 1987

as part of the Thirty Minute Theatre series

with the following cast:

A Man....................Basil Moss

A Woman.........Judy Franklin

Directed by David Johnston

THE LONG GOODNIGHT KISS

A moment of silence. FX page being turned, then FX of a toilet being flushed in the distance. A door is opened and closed. The Man yawns loudly by door.

SHE - (*in bed*) Are you coming to bed?

HE - No. I thought I would go for a midnight jog through the park in my pyjamas.

SHE - There's no need to be sarcastic. You're not very good at it anyway.

HE - Then don't ask questions to which the answers are perfectly obvious.

He removes his dressing gown. She bursts out laughing.

HE - What's so funny? Certainly not that book you're reading. Danielle Steele is never even remotely amusing.

SHE - (*still giggling*) Those pyjamas...

HE - You have had a giggle over these pyjamas every night for the past two months.

SHE - You look so ridiculous in them.

HE - These are the ones you liked, the ones you picked out for me because you found my old ones so hilarious.

SHE - Oh, they were preposterous.

HE - Well?

SHE - Maybe it's just you. Maybe it's that sweet little middle-aged paunch you're developing.

HE -   I'm glad I'm still able to entertain you after all this time.

SHE - Come to bed.

FX: She turns another page of her book.

HE -   Shall I leave my socks on?

SHE - Don't be so horrible.

HE -   (*approaching*) I wouldn't dream of it. There's too much competition.

FX: Sheetery as he gets into bed and tries to settle down.

SHE - Your feet are cold.

HE -   I offered you my socks.

SHE - Give us a kiss.

HE -   Just one?

SHE - A minimum of one.

He kisses her lightly.

SHE - Now go to sleep.

HE -   Yes, ma'am.

FX: Sheetery as he turns over once or twice. Pause. She turns a page in her book.

SHE - Are you asleep yet?

HE -   Of course not.

SHE - Why not?

HE -   You know I can never get to sleep while you're still reading your book.

SHE - You mean you can't fall asleep without the security of having me cuddled up next to you?

HE - I mean I find it difficult to fall asleep with that light on. I find it equally difficult to fall asleep while you're clattering your coffee cup and rustling the pages of your book. On top of which, I am kept awake by the eternal fear and suspense of whether the ash is going to fall from your cigarette and set fire to the bed.

SHE - Don't be stupid.

HE - I don't know why I try to go to bed at a reasonable time because I invariably end up twisted into an uncomfortable position facing this incredibly grotesque wallpaper.

SHE - You can't blame me for the wallpaper. I didn't choose it.

HE - I never said you did.

SHE - Then why bring it up?

HE - Forget the wallpaper. Can we just put the light out and go to sleep?

SHE - You go to sleep. I want to finish this chapter first.

FX: She turns another page.

HE - Is it a long chapter?

SHE - Not particularly. But you know what a slow reader I am.

HE - Maybe I should just go into the sitting room and open up the sofa bed.

SHE - Maybe you should. Maybe we should move into a larger flat so that we can have separate bedrooms. Does that idea appeal to you?

HE - It's just that...

SHE - Go sleep in the sitting room if you want to. But don't come crawling back in here when the noise from the street disturbs you or the cat jumps on top of you.

HE - I'm not going to sleep in the sitting room.

SHE - You know I can't go to sleep without reading for a bit. It helps to relax me.

HE - Yes, but an hour and a half every night...

SHE - There are other ways to relax me.

Slight pause. He turns over.

HE - Goodnight.

Another pause. She begins to noisily flip through the pages of her book.

SHE - This book is a load of rubbish.

HE - I thought you liked rubbish.

SHE - Well written rubbish, yes, but this is such unbelievable rubbish.

HE - Must be the story of my life.

She moves closer to him.

SHE - (*whispering*) I'm not going to finish this chapter or the book. I don't think I could bear another paragraph, another sentence, another word.

HE - Good. Then you can put out the light.

SHE - You prefer darkness, don't you?

HE - At times like this, yes. It helps to create the atmosphere of it being night.

SHE - (*closer to him*) Are you going to make love to me?

HE - We just made love.

SHE - When?

HE - The other night.

SHE - Was it good?

HE - It was…indescribable.

SHE - Make love to me again.

HE - In these pyjamas?

SHE - I'll close my eyes.

HE - No, thank you. The last time you did that, you fell asleep – just when I had reached the point of being totally awake.

SHE - I did not.

HE - It's nearly midnight.

SHE - How can you think about time in the midst of passion?

HE - We're not in the midst of passion. We're a long way from the midst of passion. By the time we get into the midst of passion, all chance of a decent night's sleep will have vanished.

SHE - You're not very romantic. But then you never were very romantic, were you?

HE - Yes, I was. And I still am.

FX: Sheetery as he gets out of bed and begins to pace about the room.

HE - But it's rather difficult to be romantic after a long hard frustrating day in an office populated with zombies, followed by half an hour on a train crowded with mindless aliens from another galaxy. After which I am treated to a delightful meal at home, served in its original wrappings from the fish and chip shop and consumed to the accompaniment of some overloud American soap opera followed by some very similar made in Britain – wave the Union Jack – rubbish. Until I finally stagger into the security of my own bedroom to be confronted by a vision in faded makeup and scrambled hair, with huge eyeglasses and a fag in the corner of its mouth, and a body covered with a wrinkled and slightly coffee-stained nightdress on which is written in colourful letter: Don't try to understand me, just love me. In the midst of all this, I am expected to be romantic. Passionate. To take amour where no man has ever dared amour before. Well, my little butterfly's antenna, I am sorry but not tonight, Josephine. Another time, fair Juliet. Forgive me, Isolde, but I am knackered.

Pause

SHE - Do you know what I think? I think you're getting old.

HE - If you're as old as you feel, then tonight I am ancient.

FX: He slowly gets back into bed.

SHE - You not the only one who works, you know.

HE - I know. I've heard all about your terrible day in that terrible office working for that terrible man. I have memorised all the gory details.

SHE - And yet I'm never too tired to...

Slight pause

HE - You know how I hate to disappoint you?

SHE - Yes.

HE - Well, if I made love to you right now, the result would be – I have no doubt – a colossal disappointment, a monumental let-down, an epic washout, a very definite whimper instead of a bang. For both of us.

SHE - Shall we just go to sleep then?

HE - That would be lovely.

SHE - Can I cuddle up to you?

HE - If you like, only please put that light out.

FX: She switches off the light and moves closer to him.

SHE - Do you love me?

HE - Yes.

SHE - Then say it.

HE - I love you.

SHE - As if you really mean it.

HE - As if I really mean it.

SHE - How much?

HE - Very much.

SHE - Millions and billions?

HE - Trillions.

SHE - That's all right then.

A pause as they both settle down.

SHE - Darling...

HE - Hmmm?

SHE - You'll wake me if I start to snore, won't you?

HE - If you dare to fall asleep before I do and start in on that bloody snoring, I swear you'll never wake up again.

SHE - Charming. As if you never snore.

HE - I don't know if I do or not. Why not let me go to sleep and we'll find out.

Pause

SHE - The cat snores sometimes.

HE - Love...

SHE - Yes?

HE - Shut up.

Pause. They each sigh and turn slightly.

SHE - Darling...

HE - What?

SHE - You seem to have got your elbow somehow...

HE - Sorry. I couldn't quite figure out what else to do with it. (*Moves about*) Better?

SHE - Much. Good night, sweet prince.

HE - The rest is silence. At least, I bloody well hope so.

Pause

SHE - Darling...

HE - Hmmm?

SHE - Have you heard anything?

HE - What? The cat? Or are they playing music next door again?

SHE - No, no. I meant – have you heard any news?

HE - Ummm...Let's see...Reagan has promised not to blow up Russia and the rest of the world until next year at the earliest. Thatcher says that's all right so long as she gets twenty-four hours' advance notice.

SHE - Stop trying to be funny. You know what I'm talking about. Have you heard anything about the divorce?

HE - The divorce?

SHE - The divorce.

HE - Yours? Or mine?

SHE - Well, either one.

HE - No, I haven't heard anything.

SHE - Why is it taking so long?

HE - You know what solicitors are like. You work for one.

SHE - You don't seem very concerned about it.

HE - Should I be? It's just a legal formality. Just going through the motions of bureaucratic red tape. It's not going to change anything.

SHE - Except that once we each get our divorce, we'll be able to marry each other.

HE - Yes. One scrap of paper for each of us means we can get a third scrap of paper to make an honest couple out of us. No more living in sin.

SHE - It doesn't bother you, does it?

HE - Living in sin? Why should it? It's a long established male fantasy and ambition to live in sin with a beautiful woman.

SHE - I wish I was beautiful.

HE - You are.

SHE - That's not what the mirror tells me.

HE - The Mirror? Don't tell me they had the cheek and the impertinence to turn you down for Page Three.

SHE - You know what I'm talking about.

HE - Darling, so far as I'm concerned, you are the loveliest creature in all East Grinstead. I'll even go so far as to say the most attractive female in Sussex. What the hell – in all the world. With your sweet face and fantastic body, I promise you that you'll always be the Page Three girl in my heart.

SHE - Don't laugh at me.

HE - I'm not laughing at you. I'm trying to tell you that I think you're gorgeous.

SHE - I'm not as pretty as your wife.

HE - No, you're nothing at all like my wife. That's why I love you so much.

SHE - I love you, too.

HE - You don't have to sound so miserable about it.

SHE - It's all been easy for you. Your wife made it very easy for you. You didn't have to walk out and leave her like I had to do with Trevor. You didn't have to tell her, you didn't have to say goodbye.

HE - Maybe not. But there was nothing that I went through that could ever be described as easy.

SHE - I'm sorry. She put you through hell, didn't she?

HE - Well, it seemed like it at the time. It was probably only a mild form of purgatory compared with what you went through.

SHE - What I went through? I was lonely, that's all. I existed in an advanced state of loneliness. I wouldn't have thought it possible to be married to someone and to still feel that lonely if I hadn't gone through it myself.

HE - It's not that rare an occurrence. A lot of married couples become strangers to one another. They sit together all evening – for days and weeks at a time – without uttering a single word. The upholders of the sacred institution of marriage in this modern age have a lot to answer for.

FX: She switches on the light.

HE - What did you do that for?

SHE - Do you still want to marry me?

HE - Look, this is a very dangerous topic of conversation to be getting involved in when it's late and we're both tired.

SHE - You don't, do you?

HE - I didn't say that.

SHE - You didn't say "yes" either. You didn't jump right in at the end of the question mark and answer "yes, I still want to marry you" with no hesitation or doubt.

HE - You're purposely misunderstanding...

SHE - You want to go back to her, don't you?

HE -   Who?

SHE -   Your wife. You want to go back to her. Well, why don't you if that's what you want. Go back to the slut. She's a wonderful woman!

HE -   Yes, she must be. Everybody seems to think so – her Greek boyfriend, her Italian lover, her Spanish gigolo, her French what the hell he

is. Unfortunately, she doesn't seem to have a similar soft spot for the home grown all-British male.

SHE -   Wave the Union Jack.

HE -   That's another problem. Most of the time my Union Jack seems to be flying at half-mast.

SHE -   I never minded.

HE -   What are we arguing about? I keep telling you that we shouldn't have these discussions when we're tired.

SHE -   But we're always tired.

Pause

SHE -   You're always tired.

HE -   Just lately, yes, I am.

SHE -   Has the novelty worn off?

HE -   Novelty?

SHE -   You and me.

HE -   There's more to us than that and you know it.

SHE -   Do I?

HE -   You're a silly old cow.

SHE - Not so much of the "old" if you don't mind.

HE - Sorry.

SHE - What for?

HE - I'm not quite sure. I seem to have upset you.

SHE - Well, that is something you're good at.

FX: She gets out of bed, moves off a little and puts on her dressing gown.

HE - Where are you going?

SHE - (*moves off room mic*) To get another cup of coffee.

FX: Opens door off

HE - (*gets up and follows off*) Good idea. I think I'll have one, too.

SHE - (*approaching kitchen mic*) But you never drink coffee at night. It keeps you awake.

HE - (*approaching kitchen mic*) Exactly. I think I'm going to need it.

FX: She takes a couple of cups from the shelf and puts them on table.

SHE - Instant?

HE - I didn't know there was any other kind.

SHE - (*moves off to sink*) There is but I don't know how to make it.

FX: She pours water into a kettle and switches it on. She opens a jar and spoons some instant coffee into the cups.

SHE - Milk?

HE -   Why not? We only live once.

SHE -   Sugar?

HE -   No, we don't want to go too far.

SHE -   Don't we? I would have thought that one of these days it might be exciting to see just how far we can go.

HE -   The problem with going too far is that afterwards it's such a long way to crawl back.

SHE -   Crawl back to what?

HE -   Normal everyday existence.

SHE -   If that's all there is to come back to, I'll have a single ticket rather than a return.

HE -   Sorry, that particular flight has been cancelled.

FX: Switches off kettle and pours boiled water into cups and stirs. There is a pause as she takes a deep swig of coffee.

HE -   I don't know how you can drink it as hot as that.

SHE -   One becomes accustomed to these things through repetition.

FX: Down cup on saucer

SHE -   Endless nights of hot coffee and cold men.

HE -   I'm not cold.

SHE -   No, you can be very warm – when you want to be.

HE -   You are in a mood tonight. Is there a full moon by any chance? Is it that time of the month already?

SHE -   There has to be more to life than this.

HE - A very popular theory. However, so far it remains unproven.

SHE - (*exploding*) Oh, shut up!

FX: *She throws cup across the room then begins to cry.*

HE - What is it? What's wrong?

SHE - Do I always have to ask you to hold me?

HE - Come here, come here...

She comes to him and as he holds her, her sobbing gradually ceases.

HE - Another coffee cup bites the dust. I'm glad you take it out on the crockery and not on me. I can just picture myself lying in pieces all over the kitchen.

SHE - Might do you good.

HE - I doubt it.

SHE - You bastard.

HE - I love those affectionate little pet names you have for me. At least you don't call me by your husband's name anymore.

SHE - That was only once.

HE - One time was too many.

SHE - (*moving away*) Oh, let me go. I'm going to make another cup of coffee.

HE - Here, have mine.

SHE - It's cold.

HE - Talk about symbolism.

SHE - You are a bastard, you know.

HE -   Yes, I know. And you're a bitch.

SHE -   Thank you.

HE -   What for?

SHE -   For not saying an "old" bitch.

FX: She pours some hot water into a cup and stirs in some instant coffee.

HE -   Shall we go back to bed?

SHE -   No. I'm not sleepy.

HE -   Funnily enough, now that you mention it, neither am I. Not anymore. I seem to have gone past the point of being thoroughly exhausted. Now I'm just...here.

SHE -   Do you have any cigarettes?

HE -   (*moves off*) In the sitting room. Come on... (*approaches room mic*) I knew that sooner or later tonight I was going to end up on this sofa. (*sits*)

SHE -   (*follows onto mic*) Sorry about all that. (*sits*)

HE -   That's all right. What's a relationship without a few ups and downs?

SHE -   Love me?

HE -   Yes. Even when I forget to say it.

They kiss lightly

SHE -   Do you still want to marry me?

HE -   (*lighting cigarette biz*) We're back to that again, are we?

SHE -   Yes. Answer me.

HE - Do I still want to marry you? In a word...I don't know.

SHE - You don't know.

HE - Look, you've only been married the one time, you're practically a novice at this game. This is my second divorce I'm going through. I'm getting a trifle discouraged.

SHE - I thought we were different.

HE - We are.

SHE - Well then?

HE - I'm quite happy the way we are and I think you're happy as well. You seem to be. Most of the time. Except when there's a full moon. But neither one of us can guarantee how long that will last. Happiness is very seldom an open-ended arrangement.

SHE - That's a very pessimistic attitude.

HE - I'm a pessimistic person, which is not an easy thing to say when your lips are half asleep.

SHE - So you don't want to get married?

HE - I didn't say that.

SHE - Then what exactly did you say? Underneath all the cheap cynicism and the failed attempts at humour?

HE - What I've been trying to say...that is, what I meant to say is that we should at least wait until we're both divorced. That could take months the way those idiot solicitors are mucking about. A lot could happen in that time. Let's wait and see how we feel when we're actually free and able to get married.

Pause

SHE - (*lighting a cigarette*) That's a very logical, carefully considered, cool and calculated way to look at it.

HE - You don't mean that as a compliment, do you?

SHE - You told me that you wanted to marry me more than anything else in the world.

HE - Yes, I did. And I also told you that I wanted to make passionate love to you every minute of the day and night. I have a tendency to exaggerate.

SHE - You told me you loved me.

HE - Bloody hell, I do love you.

SHE - Prove it.

HE - Darling, if I thought I possibly could, I would.

Pause

SHE - Do we have anything to drink?

HE - You've just made coffee.

SHE - No, something to drink.

HE - I think there's some whiskey...

SHE - Could I have some?

He gets up and moves over to drinks cupboard.

HE - I suppose so. (*opens cupboard and gets whiskey bottle*) You don't usually...

SHE - Just a little bit. Please.

He pours a drink and moves back to her.

HE - Here you are.

SHE - Thank you.

HE - Not at all.

He moves back to cupboard.

HE - I think I'll have one myself.

He pours another drink.

SHE - I gave up everything for you. My husband, my house, my friends, everything except my cat. All for you. But I'm still not certain what I've got in exchange. A lover? Another husband? Or a one night stand that has somehow managed to go on for nearly a year? I don't know. At least when I was still with Trevor I knew where I was. It was boring, my God, it was boring. Almost like playing the same walk-on part in a play every night for ten years. But at least I knew what was happening. I could tell which day of the week it was by the supper I was cooking and the weekends were recognised by Trevor's sleeping in late and the carefully rationed and unemotional lovemaking on Sunday afternoons. But at least I understood the situation. I knew what to expect. In nearly ten years of being married to Trevor, there was never once the single slightest surprise of any sort. None. I suppose it was all a kind of security. And when you're a woman in your mid-thirties, you begin to appreciate little abstract things like security.

HE - I never asked you to leave your husband.

SHE - You didn't have to. I volunteered. It was like losing my virginity all over again. That's a curious expression – to lose one's virginity. Makes it sound like you misplaced it in a railway station or somewhere.

HE - I lost mine in the back of a mini. That nearly cured me of sex. I couldn't stand up properly for a week.

SHE -   I didn't lose my virginity. I gave it away, with open arms.

HE -   Well, Trevor must have had a few sparks to him at some point.

SHE -   It wasn't Trevor.

HE -   Oh?

SHE -   It was...someone else.

HE -   Don't tell me – the one true love of your life.

SHE -   Something like that.

HE -   So what happened to him?

SHE -   He...died.

HE -   I'm sorry.

SHE -   Everybody was sorry. (*pause*) Can I have another drink?

HE -   I'm afraid there isn't any left. Not that there was much to start with, but you know how selfish and greedy I am.

SHE -   Just as well. If I had another drink, I might end up telling you all my secrets.

HE -   Do you have many secrets?

SHE -   Enough, although not as many as you.

HE -   I don't have any secrets.

SHE -   No, you just don't talk very much about yourself. Whenever you're in danger of revealing a bit of yourself, you somehow manage to turn it into a joke.

HE -   What do you want to know?

SHE - All sorts of things.

HE - Such as?

SHE - What do you want out of life?

HE - What does anybody want?

SHE - See what I mean?

HE - Sorry. Force of habit.

SHE - Bastard.

HE - You don't like me very much at the moment, do you?

SHE - No. But I love you.

HE - Well, that's something, isn't it?

SHE - I wasn't looking for someone to become involved with when I met you.

HE - That's the way it is, isn't it? When you want to fall in love, it's damn near impossible.

SHE - No, I definitely did not want to fall in love with you.

HE - Must have been my after shave. You hadn't seen my pyjamas at that point.

SHE - I suppose it was because you and Trevor are so different. He's always so serious but you can always make me laugh without even trying. I only joined that amateur theatre group because I wanted something to do. Something different. Sex was the last thing on my mind – it usually is when you live with someone like Trevor. But there you were, with your idiotic grin, teasing all the girls and trying to pretend you were ten years younger than you are. I thought you were the most ridiculous sight I had ever seen. Until that evening we all went out for drinks after a rehearsal and you decided, for some insane reason, to turn your charm in my direction. I admit I was flattered. I remember smiling uncontrollably. But I still don't know how I ended up in your bed that first night. I only remember that it was something I wanted to do more than anything else and that it was unbelievably marvellous. I went home in the early hours of that morning and I looked at Trevor, fast and contentedly asleep in our bed, and I thought: it's not too late to change. It is possible to have what I want.

HE -   And what do you want?

SHE -   To feel the way I felt that morning – every morning.

HE -   To dream the impossible dream.

SHE -   It's only impossible if you let it be.

HE -   You're starting to sound like those rubbishy books you read.

SHE -   If you didn't want to hear the answer, you shouldn't have asked the question.

HE -   Love, all I wanted was to get some sleep tonight.

SHE -   Well then, I suppose neither of us has got what we want.

A lengthy and awkward pause

SHE -   There's a very obvious something that you could say at this particular moment.

HE -   (*clumsily*) I'm sorry.

SHE -   (*moves off to bedroom*) That wasn't it.

HE -   (*calls off*) What are you doing?

He gets up and moves off with an exasperated exclamation. He approaches bedroom mic.

HE -   What are you doing?

SHE -   (*dressing*) I thought it was quite apparent – I'm getting dressed.

HE -   But why?

SHE -   I cannot take it anymore.

HE -   What are you talking about?

SHE -   I'm leaving.

HE -   Leaving.

SHE -   Look it up in the dictionary if you don't understand the word.

HE -   I understand the word. It's you and what you're doing and what you're babbling on about that I don't understand.

SHE -   I'm leaving. Now. Tonight.

HE -   Don't be stupid. It's after midnight.

SHE -   Don't call me stupid. I can read a clock, thank you very much. The only stupid thing I ever did was to move in with you. Our little lust nest. Well, I'm getting out now. I can't bear to wait until morning.

HE -   Where are you going to go, if one may politely inquire?

SHE -   I'll ring Trevor. (*moves off*) He'll come and fetch me. (*approaches sitting room mic*) He'd give anything to have me back. He said so.

She picks up telephone on mic.

HE - (*off in sitting room doorway*) That was last year.

SHE - (*dialling*) You wait and see. (*a beat*) It's ringing.

HE - (*still in doorway*) Thank you, British technology.

Pause

SHE - It's still ringing.

HE - I expect he's playing hard to get.

She suddenly slams the receiver down.

HE - What's the matter? (*approaches mic*) He hasn't installed an answering machine, has he? I never could stand those things...

SHE - Shut up.

HE - (*kindly*) No...tell me...

SHE - (*trying not to sob*) A woman answered the phone. Only she wasn't so much a woman as...

HE - A girl?

SHE - A girl.

HE - Well, well...

SHE - What's that supposed to mean?

HE - After all these years, Trevor finally had a surprise for you.

Her sobbing increases.

HE - You're not going to cry, are you?

SHE - No, of course I'm not going to cry. What have I got to cry about?

HE - That's what I was wondering.

SHE - You men are all alike.

HE - So are women. It's a convenient arrangement.

SHE - Fancy wasting tears on any of you lot.

HE - Would you like a cup of coffee?

SHE - Yes, as a matter of fact, I would.

HE - Just be a minute.

He moves off to kitchen where the sounds of coffee making are again heard.

SHE - (*blowing her nose*) I'm not crying because of him or whatever it is he may or may not have done. I'm crying because it still seems to matter. It still seems to matter. It still hurts. And I don't know why.

HE - (*still in kitchen*) You did love him at one time, didn't you?

SHE - Of course I did. Just as, I imagine, you loved each of your wives when you married them. I suppose that, for some people, falling in love is very easy. It's the process of falling out of love that's difficult and prolonged. And, apparently, something that is never entirely achieved.

HE - (*approaching*) Life goes on, as they say. Despite the memories, good or bad.

SHE - That's a remarkably sincere observation, coming from you.

HE - Probably something I read or overheard. Here's your coffee.

FX: Puts mug on table.

SHE - Thanks.

HE - And a cigarette.

Pause as he lights the cigarette for her with lighter.

SHE - (*inhaling deeply*) You are getting to know me rather well, aren't you?

HE - I hope so.

She takes a long drink of coffee.

SHE - That's good.

He sits down next to her.

HE - Can you imagine what the world would be like without coffee and cigarettes and alcohol?

SHE - And sex?

HE - Hardly worth living.

SHE - Is that some more of your borrowed philosophy?

HE - No, that's one of my own. The sort of thing that comes into my head on the train on my way home. (*pointedly*) Or late at night when I can't sleep.

SHE - Why don't you go to bed if that's what you want?

HE - What are you going to do?

SHE - I'm going to sit here and finish my coffee.

HE - I'll wait for you.

SHE - For God's sake, go to bed. I'm not going to do anything more foolish than to have this cigarette and this cup of coffee. I promise not to slash my wrists or take an overdose of birth control pills.

HE - Just so long as you're all right.

SHE - I'm fine.

He rises but does not leave.

HE - I suppose you may as well get undressed.

SHE - Why?

HE - You not going anywhere now, are you?

SHE - No.

HE - Besides, I like your body.

SHE - Are you trying to be nice to me?

HE - Yes.

SHE - Well, just don't, that's all.

HE - I shall never understand women.

SHE - No, I don't think you ever will.

HE - But I won't stop trying.

She rises and begins to undress.

SHE - I'm going to start looking for a flat of my own tomorrow morning.

HE - You can't do that.

SHE - Why not?

HE - Well, for one thing, you have to go to work.

SHE - I'll phone in and say I have flu.

HE - I don't want you to leave.

SHE - Don't you?

HE - I do love you, you know.

SHE - Why?

HE - I wish I knew.

SHE - I won't move too far away. We can always keep in touch. I'll remember your birthday if you'll remember mine.

HE - (*quiet and awkward*) We could always get married.

SHE - Is that a proposal?

HE - I'm not sure.

SHE - I thought women were supposed to be the ones who could never make up their minds.

HE - I wish you wouldn't undress in front of me when I'm trying to have a serious conversation with you.

SHE - All right, I'll go into the bedroom and slip into your favourite costume – black knickers and one of your dress shirts. (*moves off to bedroom*) Unbuttoned, of course.

HE - No...don't...

SHE - (*stops*) Well?

HE - I feel like Groucho Marx. (*Groucho imitation*) Say you'll marry me and you'll never see me again.

SHE - No. (*approaches mic*) Do it properly.

HE - Down on one knee?

SHE - Definitely.

He groans as he gets down on knee.

HE - My knees aren't as young as they used to be.

SHE - Neither is the rest of you.

HE - Will you marry me?

SHE - Yes, please.

HE -   Can I get up now?

SHE -   Only if you give me a kiss.

Grunting as she helps him to his feet and they kiss.

HE -   Of course, we'll have to wait until the divorces are final.

SHE -   I don't mind waiting. Not now.

HE -   Church or registry office?

SHE -   Whichever is less painful.

HE -   Suicide is generally considered to be less painful than marriage. And quicker.

SHE -   You bastard.

HE -   You bitch.

They kiss again.

SHE -   I wonder what time it is.

HE -   It's ridiculously late. Shall we go to bed?

SHE -   I won't be able to sleep.

HE -   Then read one of your books.

SHE – I've read all my books. They're all rubbish. All about people in love who make love all the time. And they all have happy endings. They're totally unrealistic. Twentieth century fiction is a load of cobblers.

HE -   So is the twentieth century.

SHE -   Give me a goodnight kiss.

HE -   I gave you one hours ago.

SHE -   You know I like long goodnight kisses.

She gives him a much longer kiss than before.

SHE - Put some music on.

HE - The neighbours won't like that.

SHE - Damn the neighbours.

HE - Right.

He moves off to player. FX: puts a cassette into the tape deck. A jazz trio plays a quiet ballad.

HE - How's that? (*approaches her*)

SHE - Lovely. (*embraces him*) Darling...

HE - Hmmm?

SHE - Wave the Union Jack.

They kiss. Bring up the jazz trio, hold, then lower under announcements.

==

ABOUT THE AUTHOR

David Kaye was born in Baltimore, Maryland in 1948. He first started to write short stories in elementary school and progressed to writing the scripts for his high school's Christmas plays and annual spring musicals. Having been bitten by the theatre bug, he went on to work at several regional repertory theatres as an assistant stage manager, a sometime actor, and the writer of workshop productions. Later on, he wrote film and music reviews for *The Chesapeake Weekly Review*. Since moving to the UK in 1984, he has written plays for BBC Radio, revue skits, and occasional magazine articles. Some of his poems were translated for publication in a Russian poetry magazine. He has recently returned to writing with renewed inspiration producing several books of both fiction and non-fiction. He now lives near London with his English wife Diane and their eccentric cat Willow.

Printed in Great Britain
by Amazon